Sorry To Hear About Your Bird

By: Colleen Hollis

Illustrated and digitized by Colleen Hollis
Copyright © 2024 Colleen's Children Line Inc. Ltd.
Publisher: Colleen's Novels Inc. Ltd.
ISBN: 978-1-964768-27-2

They require so much love,
attention and care.

Not just anyone could have raised a beautiful bird like yours.

There are many responsibilities that come with having a feathered friend. Like cleaning the cage, feeding them, and giving them water.

Can't forget how much they need play time either.

You have done such a good job caring for your feathered friend.

You have always made sure it has been taken care of to the best of your ability.

It may have been a lot of work, but you made it look easy.

If you could ask your feathered friend, I know it would say thank you for caring!

From the beginning you two
have been inseparable.

Where you were, your buddy was right by your side.

I am so sorry you have to go through this.

It is never easy to say goodbye
to our feathered friends.

We understand that it can be hard right now to think of your precious friend.

We know your pal would say
you were the best friend a bird
could have had.

When you are ready to talk about anything I am here to listen.

As you think of the love you shared, remember the bond you have could never be broken.

With time and support, I promise you will be able to think back on the memories you have made together and smile.

No matter how near or far you are, your friend remains ever present in your heart.

You are forever and always loved.

Love,_____

Friend's Facts

Friend's Name:_____

Friend's Age:_____

Friend's Favorite Food/s:_____
_____

Friend's Favorite Activity:_____
_____

Friend's Favorite Toy/s: _____
_____

Friend's Favorite Person/s:_____
_____

Feel free to write a little note, or share a memory or two.

Sorry To Hear About Your Bird, is one of the books in the children's line from Colleen's Bereavement Line For Children. Colleen's Bereavement Line for Children is aimed to assist in the healing process of children that find themselves navigating the loss of a loved one or pet. Sorry To Hear About Your Bird focuses specifically on those with a bird friend.

A name can be added to the beginning of the book, while in the back of the book there is space to write memories about the feathered friend. Followed by a page for "Friend Facts" that can be filled in for a more personal feel.

All animal books in the series are interactive as well, they are in a coloring book format. Art has been shown as a useful tool that can aid in the healing process.